Priest as Prophet

Priestly Participation in the Prophetic Ministry of Jesus

Ralph Martin, STD

Institute for Priestly Formation

IPF Publications

INSTITUTE FOR PRIESTLY FORMATION

IPF Publications
2500 California Plaza
Omaha, Nebraska 68178-0415
www.IPFPublications.com

Printed in the United States of America
ISBN-13: 978-1-7342-831-2-9

Cover design by Timothy D. Boatright
Vistra Communications
Tampa, Florida

INSTITUTE FOR PRIESTLY FORMATION

MISSION STATEMENT

In collaboration with Catholic seminaries and dioceses,
we form seminarians, priests, and bishops in holiness
and accompany them in their ongoing spiritual growth,
so they can more effectively lead others to Christ.

INSTITUTE FOR PRIESTLY FORMATION
Creighton University
2500 California Plaza
Omaha, Nebraska 68178-0415
www.priestlyformation.org
ipf@creighton.edu

PRIEST AS PROPHET
PRIESTLY PARTICIPATION IN THE PROPHETIC MINISTRY OF JESUS

The priest's sharing in the priestly, prophetic, and kingly ministry of Jesus is well known, but more attention needs to be paid to the full meaning of Jesus's prophetic ministry in order to respond effectively to the challenges the Church is facing today, both in its engagement with the culture and in the challenges of internal purification.[1] Because of the ministry challenges that the Church is facing today, we need to bring to the fore the implications of sharing in Christ's prophetic ministry in a way that we have not done before by emphasizing another priestly identity, that of priest as prophet.

I will argue that part of the huge sea of change that is required to move from "maintenance to mission"[2] and fully embrace the continuing papal calls to a "new evangelization" and the formation of "missionary disciples" is developing

1

more explicitly the identity of the priest as prophetic speaker of God's Word and doer of Spirit-inspired deeds, embodying prophetic virtues and lifestyle. When we read in Ephesians 4 about the leadership gifts the risen and ascended Christ gives to His Church, we read about apostles, prophets, pastors, teachers, and evangelists; but among these, very little attention has been paid to the priest's participation in the prophetic ministry of Jesus. Configuration to Jesus must and does include configuration to the prophetic ministry of Jesus, but the full meaning of this concept is seldom or never unfolded. Not all priests will share equally in this "five-fold" leadership constellation, but all priests need to understand and value each of these functions and participate in them according to each one's capacity.[3] The priest's configuration to the prophetic mind and heart of Jesus is not just a matter of giving sound teaching and preaching well-crafted and orthodox homilies that are not too long. Since configuration to Jesus is commonly acknowledged as an important way of understanding the purpose of seminary formation, as well as post ordination ongoing formation, let us examine what configuration to Jesus as prophet might mean. I suggest that when we examine the prophetic ministry of Jesus, we will see "virtues in action" that are particularly needed to confront the cultural and ecclesial situations we are facing today, that need to be explicitly focused on in our formation processes and cultivated in ongoing formation after ordination.

First of all, it must be said that Jesus's prophetic ministry was not a minor aspect of His ministry. When He asked His disciples who people said He was, they replied: "Some say John the Baptist, others Elijah, still others Jeremiah or one of the prophets" (Mt 16:14). People were not saying He was the new David or the new Solomon or the new Aaron—they perceived Him as a prophet, probably because of His bold and direct speech and freedom from the fear of offending people (showing no partiality to anyone),[4] as well as His prophetic deeds (signs and wonders) and His "stripped down" lifestyle, celibacy, simplicity, single-minded focus on His mission, and zeal for His Father's glory.[5]

When Jesus entered Jerusalem in the week leading up to His passion, He was primarily thought of as a prophet. "And when he entered Jerusalem, the whole city was shaken and asked, 'Who is this?' And the crowds replied, 'This is Jesus the prophet, from Nazareth in Galilee.'" (Mt 21:10-11) When the Pharisees tried to arrest Him, "they feared the crowds, for they regarded him as a prophet." (Mt 21:46) The signs that Jesus did reinforced in peoples' minds His identity as a prophet. After raising the widow's son from the dead, "Fear seized them all, and they glorified God, exclaiming, 'A great prophet has arisen in our midst,' and 'God has visited his people'" (Lk 7:16). The woman at the well, struck to the heart by Jesus's supernatural knowledge of her past, perceived Him

3

as a prophet: "Sir, I can see that you are a prophet" (Jn 4:19). After Jesus fed the five thousand, people recognized Him as the one who was fulfilling Moses's prophesy about the prophet who was to come: "This is truly the Prophet, the one who is to come into the world" (Jn 6:14). After Jesus spoke of the living waters, in anticipation of the future gift of the Holy Spirit, His listeners respond: "Some in the crowd who heard these words said, 'This is truly the Prophet'" (Jn 7:40). When the Pharisees interrogated the man born blind whom Jesus healed about who he thought Jesus was, he replied: "He is a prophet." (Jn. 9:17)

Even major figures in the history of salvation, such as David or Moses, who are seen primarily as sharers in the kingly or governing ministry, are seen also to share in the prophetic ministry and mission. Peter, in his Pentecost speech, identifies David as a prophet: "But since he was a prophet and knew that God had sworn an oath to him that he would set one of his descendants upon his throne, he foresaw and spoke of the resurrection of the Messiah" (Acts 2:30-31). Moses spoke of another prophet who would arise in the future, foretelling the coming of Christ. "A prophet like me will the Lord your God, raise up for you from among your own kindred; that is the one to whom you shall listen." (Dt 18:15) Peter cites this promise as being fulfilled in Jesus. "Moses said: 'A prophet like me will the Lord, your God, raise up for you from among your own kinsmen; to him you shall listen in all that he may say to you. Everyone who does not listen to that prophet will be cut off from the people.' . . . God raised up his servant and sent him to bless you by turning each of you from your evil ways" (Acts 3:22-26). Stephen, in his evangelistic preaching, quotes the same promise of Moses, about the coming prophet, fulfilled in Jesus.[6]

One way of getting to know better the prophetic nature of Jesus's ministry would be to meditate on the character and mission of John the Baptist, Elijah, and Jeremiah, since this is how people who encountered Jesus most frequently perceived Him. Although such a full consideration is not possible here, we can identify a few things these prophetic figures who reminded people of Jesus had in common. All of them were "outside of the camp" in some significant way, although deeply connected to friends and fellow disciples who shared their awe of the holiness of God, with a deep grasp of the true meaning of the Jewish tradition, and bearers of the prophetic tradition. They also were all recognized as being deeply connected to God, with the anointing of the Holy Spirit resting on them. All of them preached a strongly "counter cultural" message that custodians of the culture hated and that brought down upon them serious persecution. All of them had a clear sense of receiving a message from God that they were under obligation to preach, similar to how Paul expressed it in communicating his own sense of call: "Woe to me if I do not preach it [the Gospel]!" (1 Cor 9:16) The Word

5

burned within them, and they knew they were accountable to God to faithfully transmit what had been given them to proclaim. Zeal, boldness, fear of the Lord, courage, willingness to endure suffering, an ascetic lifestyle, and sensitivity to the guidance of the Spirit characterized their lives and missions.

Jesus Himself applied the designation of prophet to Himself in His encounter with the people of His hostile "native place." The people were scandalized by his ordinariness. Jesus compared His situation to that of Elijah and Elisha who did miracles only for a relatively few people (only one widow in Zarephath and only one leper, Naaman the Syrian). "Amen, I say to you, no prophet is accepted in his own native place" (Lk 4:24). "Filled with fury" (Lk 4:28), they drove Him out of the town and attempted to throw Him off the top of the hill.[7] When some Pharisees tried to warn Jesus about Herod's plan to kill Him and urged Him not to go to Jerusalem, Jesus replied: "Yet I must continue on my way today, tomorrow, and the following day, for it is impossible that a prophet should die outside of Jerusalem" (Lk 13:33).

Jesus did not speak like scholars and theologians; He did not survey learned opinions but spoke with remarkable authority.[8] Jesus did not try to win friends and influence people by softening His message. He did not avoid necessary conflict, yet He did not seek to provoke it in an untimely way.[9] He was willing for people to walk away rather than compromise the truth.[10] He did not come to work out a *modus vivendi*

6

with the ruling authorities of either the religion or the state. He did not try to preserve the reputation of the institution or of its unworthy leaders but insisted on interior righteousness as well as exterior conformity.[11] He was totally focused on His mission "to seek and to save what was lost" (Lk 19:10). His kingdom was not of this world, but He knew His disciples needed to learn how to be in it but not of it.[12] He also knew, as one of His disciples would later teach clearly, that the desire to be on friendly terms with the world may lead us to become enemies of God. "Adulterers! Do you not know that to be a lover of the world means enmity with God? Therefore, whoever wants to be a lover of the world makes himself an enemy of God" (Jas 4:4). It is sad to see that so many in the Church are still trying to be friends with the world in a way that is silencing the Gospel, some even, in the process, becoming an enemy of God.

Jesus knew salvation for mankind would take total sacrifice, even to the death, and bluntly upbraided Peter when he tried to dissuade Jesus from going to the Cross.[13] Jesus set His face toward Jerusalem, "like flint" (Is 50:7), knowing what would happen to Him there. When His disciples attempted to characterize what drove Jesus, they hearkened back to the prophet Elijah, recognizing the fiery zeal of Elijah manifested in the zeal of Jesus. "I have been most zealous for the Lord, the God of hosts" (1 Kgs 19:10).[14]

Jesus resolutely chose to go to the Temple and fulfill His destiny as the one who would save Israel.

> In the temple he found those who were selling oxen and sheep and pigeons, and the money changers at their business. And making a whip of cords, he drove them all, with the sheep and oxen, out of the temple; and he poured out the coins of the money-changers and overturned their tables. And he told those who sold the pigeons, "Take these out of here, and stop making my Father's house a marketplace." His disciples recalled the words of Scripture, "Zeal for your house will consume me." (Jn 2:16-17)

Jesus would not tolerate desecration of His Father's house. Nor would His apostles treat lightly the desecration of the new temple, the Body of Christ, by sexual immorality. Saint Paul said, "Do you not know that you are the temple of God, and that the Spirit of God dwells in you? If anyone destroys God's temple, God will destroy that person. For the temple of God, which you are, is holy" (1 Cor 3:16-17). Saint Paul also said, "Do you not know that your bodies are members of Christ? Shall I then take Christ's members and make them members of a prostitute? Of course not! . . . Avoid immorality. Every other sin a person commits is outside the body, but the immoral person sins against his own body. Do you not know that your body is a temple of the holy Spirit within you, whom you have from God, and that you are not your own? For you have been purchased at a price. Therefore, glorify God in your body" (1 Cor. 6:15-20).[15]

Nor would Jesus tolerate causing little ones (children, disciples, believers, the new temple of God) to be scandalized and fall: "Whoever receives one child such as this in my name receives me. Whoever causes one of these little ones who believe in me to sin, it would be better for him to have a great millstone hung around his neck and to be drowned in the depth of the sea. Woe to the world because of things that cause sin! Such things must come, but woe to the one through whom they come!" (Mt. 18:5-7)[16]

Serious sin is such a grave offense to God and so endangers people's eternal salvation that Jesus urges that the most extreme measures necessary to avoid sin and damnation be taken. "And if your hand or your foot causes you to sin, cut it off and throw it from you; it is better for you to enter life maimed or lame than with two hands or two feet to be thrown into the eternal fire. And if your eye causes you to sin, pluck it out and throw it from you; it is better for you to enter life with one eye than with two eyes to be thrown into the hell of fire" (Mt. 18:8-9). He was especially angered, as were the Old Testament prophets, by religious leadership that was corrupt, unfaithful, and spiritually blind, operating by worldly wisdom, controlled by political expediency, favoring the rich at the expense of the poor, motivated by self-love.

Jesus was deadly serious about His mission and message. He wept; He shouted; He rebuked; He insulted; He condemned. He admonished, warned, and urged with passion. He longed for "fire" to be kindled on the earth (Lk 12:49). He almost always challenged people to make a decision to believe in Him, to follow Him, to obey Him—or not. He frequently pointed out the eternal consequences of people's choices in relationship to Him. He asked for total commitment and gave it in return.

Peter Kreeft's characterization of the encounter with the real Jesus as "Jesus shock" is very apt.[17] Jesus lived in the light of what He knew of the coming judgment and of the certain and eternal division of the human race into the saved and the lost, based on their response to Him and the grace of God. He was a man on a mission, single-mindedly advancing it every day, continually warning people about the eternal consequences if they rejected the "rescue mission" He was undertaking. As Jesus asked on one occasion: "Does this shock you?" (Jn 6:61)

Of course, focusing on the configuration of the priest to the prophetic dimension of Jesus and His prophetic words, actions, and emotions does not give us a complete picture of Jesus; but that is not the purpose of this book. The purpose of this book is to supplement the excellent work that has been done on showing configuration to Jesus as priest, shepherd, and head (and the various specifications of these identities by the Institute for Priestly Formation as Beloved Son, Chaste Spouse, Good Shepherd, Spiritual Father, and Spiritual Physician) by showing what configuration to the prophetic identity of Christ can effectively accomplish and what virtues it can instill in filling out the picture of priestly identity. I would now like to identify some of the important virtues or character traits that we find in Jesus's prophetic identity and then briefly sketch how each dimension of formation, and of continuing formation, needs to be reviewed to make sure that it adequately incorporates the prophetic dimension of Jesus's ministry and the concomitant virtues.

Prophetic Virtues

Among the prophetic virues are the following: fear of the Lord; zeal for the holiness of God and His house; zeal for the salvation of souls; righteous anger at those who would cause little ones (disciples, believers) to be scandalized; courage in confronting the powerful with the truth of their situation and a call to repentance; boldness in proclaiming the message without compromise; a contemplative intensity informed by knowledge of the shortness of life, the impending judgment, and the one thing necessary. This book will focus on this complex of virtues under the primary heading of the virtue of zeal.

Zeal is created through a confluence of knowledge and love and results in a single-hearted desire to take every opportunity to foster the salvation of souls[18] and the honor and glory of God. Enthusiasm may wax and wane, but zeal is a deeply rooted conviction and determination to do all for the glory of God and the good of souls. Fortitude, steadfastness, and determination are all allied virtues and character traits that are linked to zeal. Regularly, in the Liturgy, the Church prays for zeal:

> O Lord, through our Easter celebrations, renew your people in zeal to speak and live the Gospel, that the Church may truly be a living sacrament of salvation for all peoples, through Christ our Lord. Amen. (Friday of the Easter Octave)

St. Thomas Aquinas argues that zeal arises from the intensity of love:

> For it is evident that the more intensely a power tends to anything, the more vigorously it withstands opposition or resistance . . . an intense love seeks to remove everything that opposes it . . . In this respect a man is said to be zealous on behalf of his friend, when he makes a point of repelling whatever may be said or done against the friend's good. In this way, too, a man is said to be zealous on God's behalf, when he endeavors, to the best of his

means, to repel whatever is contrary to the honor or will of God; according to 1 Kings 19:14 "With zeal I have been zealous for the Lord of hosts." Again on the words of John 2:17: "The zeal of your house has eaten me up."[19]

Godly zeal, of course, is not simply a blind energy or enthusiasm; it must be enlightened by wisdom and form part of a constellation of virtues that together go to make a mature and balanced character, according to the current four dimensions of priestly formation.

As Saint Paul said in relation to the zealous Jews of his time, perhaps reflecting back on his own zeal as a Pharisee, "they have zeal for God, but it is not discerning" (Rom 10:2). But Paul did not lack in zeal once he encountered Jesus and plumbed the depths of His Gospel. What was said of Elijah—and Jesus—could equally be said of Paul. Nevertheless, I think zeal is a virtue that is often lacking in the response I see being made to the persistent call of the Church to a new evangelization and of Pope Francis's call to form missionary disciples, and needs to be consciously fostered in our formation programs, not just on the level of theological understanding or "virtue theory" but on the affective level as well. I also see zeal lacking in the response of many priests and bishops to the horrendous crisis in which we are currently involved. The zeal of Elijah was clearly a virtue that permeated his whole being—including a contemplative knowledge of the holiness of God, the gravity of infidelity to God, and the God-given impulse to speak a prophetic word into the situation and the courage to do so despite certain serious opposition. One, indeed, might say that zeal is a necessary component of the priest's participation in the prophetic ministry of Jesus and one that is uniquely needed for evangelization and missionary discipleship.

Intellectual Formation and Prophetic Zeal

There is knowledge that is needed as a foundation for zeal—knowledge of the holiness of God; knowledge of the purpose of creation (union with God); knowledge of the gravity and horror of sin; knowledge of the just punishment for sin (eternal separation from God); knowledge of the stupendous act of love in Creation, Redemption, and participation in Trinitarian life, in the very nature of God, for all eternity. Clear theological (rational) understanding of these realities is essential but so is an affective and contemplative appropriation in ever deepening ways. Saint Paul's exhortation to Timothy to "Reflect on what I am saying, for the Lord will give you understanding in everything" (2 Tm 2:7) reveals the expected interplay between rational thought and illumination brought by the Holy Spirit.

Theological Deceptions That Undermine Zeal

I would like to pick out two intellectual/theological deceptions that undermine zeal for holiness, evangelization, and the sacrifice of priestly vocations which, if corrected, combined with deeper contemplative insight, would serve to increase appropriate zeal. The first is the presumption that virtually everyone will be saved. The second is that the Church needs to accommodate people where they are in the realm of sexuality.

The Presumption that Virtually Everyone Will Be Saved

Theological ambivalence about whether hell could be a realistic outcome for people removes one major intellectual component that fueled Jesus's zeal. In fact, I would say that it is Jesus's profound vision of what is at stake for every human being—heaven or hell—that was a primary motivator not only of his prophetic and evangelistic zeal, but of the whole plan of salvation. Unfortunately, if I were to describe how very many of our fellow Catholics look at these matters today, I would describe it like this: "Broad and wide is the way that leads to salvation/heaven, and almost everybody is on that way. Narrow and difficult is the path that leads to condemnation/hell; and very few, if any, are on that road." Sometimes, it is conceded that particularly bad people like Hitler or Stalin may be in hell.

Now, the problem with this way of looking at things is that it is the exact opposite of what Jesus tells us about our situation in the Gospel. "Enter through the narrow gate; for the gate is wide and the road broad that leads to destruction, and those who enter through it are many. How narrow and constricted the road that leads to life. And those who find it are few" (Mt 7:13-14). Or, one might consider a parallel passage in Luke: "Someone asked him, 'Lord, will only a few people be saved?' He answered them, 'Strive to enter through the narrow door, for many, I tell you, will attempt to enter but will not be strong enough'" (Lk 13:23-24). Now Jesus did not say these things because this is how things have to be or because this is how He wants them to be but simply because this is how things were when He looked out at the situation of the Jewish people in His time. And are our times any better?

Perhaps, at certain high points of Christian culture, "many" were on the way to salvation, and "fewer" on the way to condemnation; but in our time, it is clear that the main river of culture is flowing ever more swiftly toward destruction. Increased anxiety, stress, the stupefying confusion about basics such as male and female identity, and the plummeting birth rate are all signs that our culture is rapidly heading in a direction that is destructive for human happiness, both here in this life and, unfortunately, unless there is repentance, in eternal life.

We also know that Jesus was brokenhearted about the prospect of so many being lost by their own choice when He wept as He foresaw their destruction on the hill overlooking Jerusalem.[20] But, some might ask, "Was this picture of salvation and damnation changed by Vatican II? Are we not to have a more positive outlook about most people being saved?" Others might ask, "Is God not so merciful that He will never let anyone be lost?" While complete answers to these questions are beyond the scope of this book, I hope it is sufficient at this time to simply note that theological clarity on this issue is essential for priestly zeal for the salvation of souls.[21]

But not only are the eternal destinies of people who have never heard the Gospel in grave jeopardy but, also, the eternal destinies of Catholics who may have been baptized and may have some self-identification as Catholics but who are not living as disciples of Christ are in jeopardy.

This is what Vatican II teaches about the situation of many Catholics:

> Even though incorporated into the Church, one who does not however persevere in charity is not saved. He remains indeed in the bosom of the Church, but "in body" not "in heart." All children of the Church should nevertheless remember that their exalted condition results, not from their own merits, but from the grace of Christ. If they fail to respond in thought, word and deed to that grace, not only shall they not be saved, but they shall be the more severely judged.[22]

Why bother to evangelize? Because the eternal destinies (heaven or hell) of many millions of our fellow Catholics—not to mention, many millions of countless others—are hanging in the balance. Christianity is not just an optional enrichment possibility for human life but a message that truly is a matter of life or death, heaven or hell. If a priest truly loves his people and those who are called to be his people, he is going to be dedicated to their salvation and pay the price that Saint John Vianney, the patron saint of priests, was willing to pay: much personal interaction where people are living and working (the smell of the sheep) and much prayer and fasting for the salvation of his flock and much "straight talk" in his sermons and conversations about the shortness of life and the coming judgement.[23]

I have personally been going through another round of "Jesus shock" as some young men in our office (who are reaching out to young adults) and I are going through a bible study focusing on what Jesus and the Apostles say about the eternal consequences of refusing to believe in Jesus or repent of sin. We are shocked at how frequent and clear such references are. And this has a specific application not only to the fog of false universalism that we have just discussed but to the second deception that undermines prophetic preaching and teaching and lifestyle, silence—or worse—on what Jesus and the Apostles teach about the purpose of God-given sexuality.

*The Presumption that the Church Needs to Accommodate People
Where They Are in the Realm of Sexuality*

The second deception that profoundly affects many of our people, as well as our priests and seminarians, is confusion, and perhaps unbelief, about the Church's teaching on sexual morality. That confusion and unbelief causes a great reluctance, even fear, on the part of clergy to speak about those things.

For many decades now, our people, and perhaps we ourselves, have heard sermons or catechesis like this: God is mainly concerned about the really important issues such as social justice, the environment, peace in the world, racial equality, and care for the poor; and He is not so much concerned about the small, personal things, including sexual morality. The Church is too hung up on sexual morality and needs to appreciate how people's view of sexuality has evolved these days. Even leading bishops and cardinals and, indeed, whole episcopal conferences serving entire countries communicate this mentality and explicitly or implicitly communicate a lack of belief in what Sacred Scripture, Sacred Tradition, and the *Catechism of the Catholic Church* teach on these personal, sexual matters.

One truly egregious example of how far this questioning the Catholic sexual ethic has gone is the state of the Catholic Church in Germany. When Pope Emeritus Benedict XVI published a lengthy analysis of the real causes of the sexual abuse and immorality crisis, reaffirming the clear teachings of Scripture and Tradition, most recently in the very important encyclical *Veritatis Splendor*, his analysis was met with virulent attacks by leading figures in the German church. Benedict pointed out that the cultural revolution of the 1960s led to a moral relativism that penetrated Catholic theology and seminaries in which there were already, in his words, "homosexual cliques." This comment by Benedict XVI was met with outrage among German moral theologians who published on the German bishops official website and in interviews with Catholic news outlets what can only be called a blatant affirmation of "unbelief" in the truth of the Church's teaching in this area. It is not hard to decipher what the upcoming Synod of the German Catholic Church has as its agenda. Cardinal Gerhard Muller, former head of the Congregation for the Doctrine of the Faith, characterizes the response of the German theologians to Pope Emeritus Benedict's essay like this: "These are people who neither believe nor think."[24]

Another form in which this deception comes is an emphasis on the mercy of God but an ignorance of His judgment. Sometimes, this deception is expressed like this: "God is merciful and will always forgive me." Of course, God is concerned about the really big things; but He is also concerned about those most personal of our actions, including the realm of sexuality, that most profoundly affect our own souls, bodies, and minds, as well as the souls, bodies, and minds of others. And, of course, God is merciful and will always forgive us if we sincerely repent and take every measure necessary not to sin anymore.

Even though some controversy has developed about whether Pope Francis is trying to "loosen things up" in the area of sexual morality, and puzzlement grows about why the German bishops and others who openly push the Church in a direction of "loosening up" sexual morality are not being strongly corrected, we need to take Pope Francis at his word that he believes everything in the *Catechism of the Catholic Church* and, even more so, take Jesus and the Apostles at their word that sinning sexually is, indeed, a serious matter and unless repented of, will likely exclude us from the Kingdom of God. The Word of God is very clear: It is not only the act of adultery that is a serious sin but giving in to lustful thoughts about adultery is a serious sin. Jesus is calling us to a higher standard than was previously known in Old Testament times, not a lower standard. And Jesus and His Apostles are consistent in their teaching about the seriousness of sexual immorality.

> You have heard that it was said, "You shall not commit adultery." But I say to you, everyone who looks at a woman with lust has already committed adultery with her in her heart. If your right eye causes you to sin, tear it out and throw it away. It is better for you to lose one of your members than to have your whole body thrown into

Gehenna. And if your right hand causes you to sin, cut it off and throw it away. It is better for you to lose one of your members than to have your whole body go into Gehenna. (Mt 5:27-30)

Persisting in sexual sin clearly endangers our salvation, and if we do not tell people that message clearly and confidently, we ourselves will be liable for judgement. "Do you not know that the unjust will not inherit the kingdom of God? Do not be deceived; neither fornicators nor idolaters nor adulterers nor boy prostitutes nor sodomites nor thieves nor the greedy nor drunkards nor slanderers nor robbers will inherit the kingdom of God" (1 Cor 6:9-10).

Sexual sins are not the only serious sins that can exclude us from the kingdom of God; but for those who are baptized, they are singled out as particularly offensive as they are sins against our own body, which is a temple of the Holy Spirit:

> Do you not know that your bodies are members of Christ? Shall I then take Christ's members and make them the members of a prostitute? Of course not! . . . Avoid immorality. Every other sin a person commits is outside the body, but the immoral person sins against his own body. Do you not know that your body is a temple of the holy Spirit within you, whom you have from God and that you are not your own? For you have been

purchased at a price. Therefore, glorify God in your body. (1 Cor 6:15-20)

This message certainly resonates with what Mary is reported as having said to Saint Jacinta on her deathbed that "more souls go to hell because of sins of impurity than any other."[25] The Apostles' warnings about the grave danger of engaging in sexual immorality are repeated many times. "Now the works of the flesh are obvious: immorality, impurity, licentiousness, idolatry, sorcery, hatreds, rivalry, jealousy, outbursts of fury, acts of selfishness, dissension, factions, occasions of envy, drinking bouts, orgies, and the like. I warn you, as I warned you before, that those who do such things will not inherit the kingdom of God" (Gal 5:19-21).

And further, "Immorality or any impurity or greed must not even be mentioned among you, as is fitting among holy ones, no obscenity or suggestive talk, which is out of place, but instead, thanksgiving. Be sure of this, that no immoral or impure greedy person, that is, an idolater, has any inheritance in the kingdom of Christ and of God. Let no one deceive you with empty arguments, for because of these things the wrath of God is coming upon the disobedient" (Eph 5:3-6).

And after the most beautiful description of the final union of God and man, the fate of the unrepentant is revealed: "But as for the cowards, the unfaithful, the depraved, murderers, the unchaste, sorcerers, idol-worshipers, and deceivers of every sort, their lot is in the burning pool of fire and sulfur, which is the second death" (Rev 21:8). As Jesus puts it: "And do not be afraid of those who can kill the body but cannot kill the soul; rather, be afraid of the one who can destroy both soul and body in Gehenna" (Mt 10:28).[26]

It is in the area of sexual morality today that clear preaching and teaching is most needed, but also much lacking. Fear, cowardice, unbelief, and sometimes bondage to sexual sin so often keeps the truly good news of the truth about human sexuality from being communicated clearly and confidently by our clergy.[27] Our culture, in its most important institutions, has largely abandoned any defense of biblical morality but rather, has launched—with all the power that elite institutions can bring to bear—an aggressive effort to enforce a relativism where "anything goes." But as Cardinal Dolan once said, for the Church, it is true that all are welcome but not that anything goes.[28]

What keeps priests from preaching clearly in this area today? First of all, fear. Not fear of hell, not fear of God, but fear of how people will react to them and what people will say about them and what price they may have to pay if they speak about these things clearly. This is also known as cowardice, and the cowardly are finally banished from God's presence and consigned to the second death, hell. How pathetic to fear what people will think of us if we tell them the truth that could save them, rather than to fear appearing before the judgement seat of Christ and have to give an account to Him!

What keeps priests from preaching clearly in this area today? A lack of love. How terrible not to have the courage to tell people the truth about what could save their souls! We all have to be willing to pay whatever price is needed to preach and teach clearly the truths that can save people, just as Jesus did. The servant is not above the master. We have to be willing to endure the same persecution as He did. But as the writer of Hebrews says, we have not yet had to pay the price of shedding our blood!

What keeps priests from preaching clearly in this area today? A lack of faith. Many priests and people through corrosive "Scripture scholarship" have lost their confidence in the truth and reliability of God's Word as it comes to us in Scripture and Tradition. Vatican II did not cast us into a sea of doubt and skepticism, and we need to recover its authentic teaching. "Since, therefore, all that the inspired authors, or sacred writers, affirm should be regarded as affirmed by the Holy Spirit, we must acknowledge that the books of Scripture, firmly, faithfully and without error, teach that truth which God, for the sake of our salvation, wished to see confided to the Sacred Scriptures."[29] As Saint Augustine puts it: "If you believe what you like in the gospels and reject what you don't like, it is not the gospel you believe but yourself."[30]

What keeps priests from preaching clearly about salvation and morality today? Sometimes, unfortunately, their own personal sin. Sad to say, it appears that a certain number of priests have themselves become ensnared in relativistic thinking and even bondage to sexual immorality. The incidence of pornography addiction, adultery, fornication, and homosexual relationships appears to be not inconsiderable in many places, sometimes combined with embezzlement to support a sinful lifestyle. While bishops, under pressure from lawyers, journalists, and the threat of financial ruin, did indeed take significant steps toward greatly reducing incidences of sexual abuse of children, there is a strange reluctance to talk about the problem of sexual immorality of other kinds among the clergy, including those purported to be with "consenting" adults, and most particularly, a reluctance to talk about homosexuality among the clergy.

Until bishops overcome their fear, their entanglement in their own emotional bondages to certain priests out of fear of offending a "classmate" or losing popularity among priests or being portrayed in the press as heartless conservatives, it will be hard for our priests to stand firm and proclaim with boldness, confidence, and joy the whole truth of the Gospel, including the truth about heaven and hell, and the truth about those sins that will exclude us from the kingdom unless they are repented of.[31] A recovery of zeal for the holiness of God's house, and for His glory, a recovery of the prophetic dimension of Jesus's ministry needs to be based on a recovery of a profound fear of God, love for His people, knowledge of the truth, and faith in the Word of God.

Knowledge of the words of Jesus and the Apostles, knowledge of what is taught in the *Catechism of the Catholic Church* is not enough, as we know, to fuel zeal. There needs to be a contemplative infusion of both love and knowledge that ignites a living flame of love and prophetic zeal. Besides a clear theological understanding of the truth about heaven and hell, salvation and damnation, a contemplative knowledge of these truths is needed, which will infuse a flame of pastoral charity that will give sustained energy to fervent preaching, teaching, and governing actions, as well as priestly sacrifice, both in the Liturgy and in personal sacrifice. I would like now to draw our attention to examples of such contemplative infusion and the results in pastoral charity and zeal.

Saint Francis Xavier

The Spiritual Exercises of Saint Ignatius often are the occasion for such infused contemplation to be experienced, prepared for by prayerful mediation on Jesus and His teaching. When Saint Francis was at his missionary post in India, he wrote to Saint Ignatius about the lack of zeal that he found at the University of Paris:

Many, many people hereabouts are not becoming Christians for one reason only: there is nobody to make them Christians. Again and again I have thought of going round the universities of Europe, especially Paris, and everywhere crying out like a madman, riveting the attention of those with more learning than charity: "What a tragedy: how many souls are being shut out of heaven and falling into hell, thanks to you!" . . . I wish they would work as hard at this as they do at their books, and so settle their account with God for their learning and the talents entrusted to them. This thought would certainly stir most of them to meditate on spiritual realities, to listen actively to what God is saying to them. They would forget their own desires, their human affairs, and give themselves over entirely to God's will and his choice. They would cry out with all their heart: Lord, I am here! What do you want me to do? Send me anywhere you like—even to India.[32]

But not every experience of the Exercises produces this zeal. No method can guarantee a contemplative infusion. As John of the Cross would say, we can only dispose ourselves for such an infusion; only God can graciously grant it, but He wants to. In my own experience of the Exercises—two eight-day retreats and one thirty-day retreat—all of which were profoundly fruitful in my own life, it was disappointing that the key meditation on hell was guided by a demythologizing meditation by Rahner that emptied it of its power.

Sister Jacinta

One of the most remarkable infusions of contemplative insight into the truths of our faith regarding heaven and hell happened to the three children at Fatima. I have been familiar with the "facts" of Fatima for virtually my whole life, but recently, I was there and experienced an "awakening" to the depth and relevance of the messages.

In 1916, an angel appeared three different times to three small children who lived in a small rural village and were at that time only six, eight, and nine years old. There was a brother and sister, Francisco and Jacinta, and their slightly older cousin, Lucy. The angel identified himself as the Angel of Portugal and the Angel of Peace and taught the children several prayers:

> My God, I believe, I adore, I hope, and I love You! I ask pardon of You for those who do not believe, do not adore, do not hope, and do not love You.[33]

The angel prayed with his forehead touching the ground and taught the children the profound reverence owed to God. They forever after often prayed like that themselves. After the first visit of the angel, they said they could hardly speak to each other so powerful were the "aftereffects" of this encounter with the supernatural. Lucy remarks that the words of the angel "were indelibly impressed on our souls."[34]

At the third visit of the angel, he taught them this prayer:

> Most Holy Trinity, Father, Son and Holy Spirit, I offer You the most precious Body, Blood, Soul, and Divinity of Jesus Christ, present in all the tabernacles of the world,

in reparation for the outrages, sacrileges and indifference with which He Himself is offended. And, through the infinite merits of His most Sacred Heart, and the Immaculate Heart of Mary, I beg of You the conversion of poor sinners.[35]

The communication, though, that I want to focus on that will cast light on our current considerations is the apparition of Mary to the children on July 13, 1917. Mary opened her hands, and the earth seemed to open beneath the children; and they saw a horrifying vision of hell with damned souls in agony and demons in hideous shapes. Terrified, they looked to Mary; and this is what she said to them:

You have seen hell where the souls of poor sinners go. To save them, God wishes to establish in the world devotion to my Immaculate Heart. If what I say to you is done, many souls will be saved and there will be peace.[36]

After showing them the reality of hell, she taught them this prayer to say after each decade of the Rosary:

O my Jesus! Forgive us our sins, save us from the fire of hell. Lead all souls to heaven, especially those in most need of Thy Mercy.[37]

In August, Mary told them:

Pray, pray very much, and make sacrifices for sinners; for many souls go to hell because there are none to sacrifice themselves and to pray for them.[38]

The vision of hell and Mary's words deeply impacted their souls, and they fervently responded to her request. Little Jacinta would often ask her brother and cousin: "Have you sacrificed for the conversion of sinners today?" They would often give their lunches to poor children, go without drinking water for long periods of time, and do other sacrifices. Mary also asked the children to offer the suffering that would come their way, as well as their voluntary prayers and sacrifices, for reparation for the sins that are so offending God and Mary. Mary also told the children that she would take Jacinta and Francisco to heaven soon but that Lucy would need to learn to read and write as she needed to stay on earth longer to witness to this message (she died in 2005 at the age of ninety-seven in a Carmelite monastery). Francisco died in 1919, not yet ten, of the flu epidemic that swept the world at that time; and Jacinta, in 1920 at the age of ten. Mary told Jacinta that if she was willing, she would suffer much and die alone in a hospital, but Mary would be with her. In a brutal operation, the doctors tried to cleanse an open fistula in her side. She was so weak she could not have general anesthesia, and the local was ineffective. She died alone in a Lisbon hospital. Jacinta and Francisco were officially proclaimed saints a few years ago at Fatima by Pope Francis, and the cause for Lucy has begun.

So, what struck me so deeply? The children. And their totally fervent, wholehearted focus on the salvation of souls and how their whole way of life and each and every day was focused on prayer and sacrifice for the conversion of sinners. It reminds me of Jesus's words: "Unless you turn and become like children, you will not enter the kingdom of heaven" (Mt 18:3). Wholehearted belief in the words spoken, wholehearted response with mind, heart, and body is needed. Monsignor John Esseff, a noted spiritual director and exorcist, in a telephone conversation, asked me what was going on in my life; and I told him about the impact of the children of Fatima. He told me that in exorcisms of children that he sometimes performed, the demons flee when a photo of Jacinta is held up to them, so powerful is her intercession and holiness.

Our seminarians need contemplative experiences like the children of Fatima to be seared on their soul, and the words of Jesus and Mary and the saints, indelibly impressed on their souls. Meditating on the Word of God on the eternal consequences of rejecting Jesus and refusing to repent of serious sin can be the occasion for such a contemplative insight and increase of pastoral charity necessary for missionary disciples. Saint Francis de Sales said that meditating on the evil of sin and what it cost in the Crucifixion of Jesus, and the eternal consequences of not repenting and living a godly life was the best means for overcoming bondage to sin.

And it is no accident that not many years later, Jesus commanded an angel to take Saint Faustina on a tour of hell so no one could say that hell does not exist and that there is no one there. Faustina's vision is terrifying and is very similar to that of Catherine of Siena over six hundred years ago and of what Mary showed the children at Fatima. The deception that God is so merciful that no one will be lost that has gripped the Church in a haze of indifferentism was intended to be blocked by the vision of hell given to Faustina and the many specific revelations contained in her diary that indicate that if there is no response to mercy with faith and repentance, many will perish and that, in fact, many are perishing.

The New Pentecost

There is a fascinating comment that Peter makes when explaining his reason for baptizing Cornelius and his household as recounted in Acts 11. "As I began to speak, the holy Spirit fell upon them as it had upon us at the beginning, and I remembered the word of the Lord, how he had said, 'John baptized with water but you will be baptized with the holy Spirit.' If then God gave them the same gift he gave to us when we came to believe in the Lord Jesus Christ, who was I to be able to hinder God?' When they heard this, they stopped objecting and glorified God, saying, 'God has

then granted life-giving repentance to the Gentiles too'"
(Acts 11:15-18).

There are many rich insights that could be commented
on in these few verses, but the comment that I want to draw
our attention to now is what Peter could possibly mean by
saying "when we believed in the Lord Jesus Christ." Did
Peter and the other disciples first believe in the Lord only
after receiving the outpouring of the Holy Spirit at Pentecost? Yes and no. They believed before but not with enough
knowledge or love to stay with Jesus in His Passion, to not
deny Him under social pressure, and not to venture freely
in the streets of Jerusalem even after His Resurrection. And
even on the day of the Ascension, they were still wondering
if Jesus was about to take over Jerusalem and rule there as
king. The apostles really did not "get it" or "get Jesus" until
after the outpouring of the Holy Spirit. They did not have the
certainty of faith or the profound, affective, rational, contemplative experience of faith and its implications until after the
Holy Spirit fell.

Let us look at one more text before drawing some conclu-
sions for our formation processes:

Then he opened their minds to understand the scriptures.
And he said to them, "Thus it is written that the Messiah
would suffer and rise from the dead on the third day and
that repentance for the forgiveness of sins, be preached
in his name to all nations, beginning from Jerusalem.

You are witnesses of these things. And [behold] I am sending the promise of my Father upon you; but stay in the city until you are clothed with power from on high" (Lk 24:45-49).

The disciples before Pentecost had the best explanation of Scripture anyone ever had. They had the best spiritual direction, character formation, and pastoral supervision; but they were sorely lacking prophetic zeal. They were "well formed" but were not ready to be missionary disciples. It was not until after Pentecost that they "got it."

When we take a look at these examples, we must admire the prophetic and rational wisdom of every pope, from Saint John XXIII up to and including Pope Francis, who fervently have prayed for and exhorted us to pray for a new Pentecost for the Church. Orthodoxy is not enough, however essential it is; correct Liturgy is not enough, however essential it is; chaste celibacy is not enough, however essential it is; what is needed in addition is the power of the Holy Spirit to bring all these wonderful fruits of formation into a living flame of love that urges on our priests with prophetic zeal.

Is it not this contemplative experience of God's presence, power, truthfulness, and love that Paul insisted needed to be at the foundation of all faith?

I came to you in weakness and fear and much trembling, and my message and my proclamation were not with persuasive (words of) wisdom, but with a demonstration of spirit and power, so that your faith might rest not on human wisdom but on the power of God. (1 Cor 2:3-4)

We need to build into our formation programs opportunities for our seminarians to appropriate this truth and to fervently desire and pray for an outpouring of the Holy Spirit on them.

This contemplative and charismatic experience of the Spirit is not supposed to be the pinnacle of the Christian life but its foundation (Baptism in the Spirit is considered by most biblical scholars to signify full incorporation into the life of Christ and the Church—focused sacramentally in the sacraments of Christian initiation). Having this experiential foundation provides a "memory" that is extremely helpful for the arduous work of the spiritual journey, including all its stages of purification, detachment, and dark nights. It does not replace the need for the traditional spiritual wisdom but provides an experiential foundation that is of great help, a "memory" that continues to encourage perseverance.

Human Formation and Prophetic Zeal

All the character formation that must take place in human formation is essential for the human foundation of prophetic zeal to be established. Prophetic zeal that is not founded on a solid character with all the virtues needed to support it and guide it in wisdom is dangerous. Everything we do to build character and instill the virtues in our seminarians is the necessary framework for the infused gifts of the Spirit to find their proper home. Basic virtues like reliability, truthfulness, humility, fortitude, perseverance, the ability to deny oneself regularly, brotherly love, and compassion are all essential for the proper operation of prophetic zeal. However, there are some human and acquired virtues that may sometimes not be emphasized enough to provide a sufficient character foundation for the proper operation of prophetic zeal. For example, courage is particularly important and is notably evident in the ministry of Jesus, courage to speak the truth even when one knows it may not be readily accepted or may even be vigorously opposed. Determination to preach the gospel in season and out of season, when it is convenient and inconvenient is an important character trait. Working with seminarians to overcome their desire to be accepted and to "please men," whether it be their parishioners, family members, big donors, fellow priests, or bishops—when it would mean displeasing God—is particularly important in our formation today. All our priests—and all Christians, for that matter—need to be decidedly in the place where they fear God more than man and are able to think, speak, and act accordingly.

A lot of the sickness in the Church today can be traced to a lack of these virtues. C. S. Lewis's insights on the powerful attraction that being part of the "inner circle" has on our fallen flesh well illustrates the importance of human formation in these virtues.

I believe that in all men's lives at certain periods, and in many men's lives at all periods between infancy and extreme old age, one of the most dominant elements is the desire to be inside the local Ring and the terror of being left outside . . . Unless you take measures to prevent it, this desire is going to be one of the chief motives of your life, from the first day on which you enter your profession until the day when you are too old to care . . . Of all the passions, the passion for the Inner Ring is most skillful in making man who is not yet a very bad man do very bad things . . . As long as you are governed by that desire you will never get what you want. You are trying to peel an onion: if you succeed there will be nothing left. Until you conquer the fear of being an outsider, an outsider you will remain.[39]

In my Licentiate in Sacred Theology class a few summers ago, with thirty priests from all over the country, the question of the "McCarrick" scandal came up, and we had a lively discussion. When I suggested that the code of silence needed to be broken and people need to start speaking up when they know sexual immorality is going on, the priests surprised me with their response. "You can't possibly understand as a layman what fear we live in." I was astounded. And this was the general consensus of the class—diocesan and religious, North American and international. They told me that they were afraid of what their superiors could do to them if they spoke up. "We could be transferred to an isolated rural parish; bad things could be put in our 'files' to be used later; we could be shunned by our fellow priests; our bishop would never favor us again; we wouldn't get the assignment that really matched our gifts," etc. These priests, for the most part, were living in a variety of fear. I told them I thought they needed an infusion of simple human courage and a good dose of the fear of the Lord so they would fear God more than man. "For God did not give us a spirit of cowardice but rather of power and love and self-control" (2 Tm 1:7). There is a culture of "cover up," of silence, of complacency, and quite frankly, of cowardice that has deeply informed many of our priests and is operating strongly in forming future priests. There is an "infantilism" that has been bred in grown men who are unable to relate as fellow human beings, brothers in Christ, in a healthy way to authority. There is a tremendous fear of conflict. Human formation needs to take all these factors into account and help people to become accustomed to speaking the truth in love to one another and to those they serve and those they serve under.

Pastoral Formation and Prophetic Zeal

Pastoral formation needs to take into account that the "big picture" includes a vivid revelation of the spiritual warfare that characterizes life on earth. If we were to really "get" what Ephesians 6:10-20 implies for pastoral ministry, we would certainly be approaching our own salvation and pastoral responsibilities with "fear and trembling." There is a spiritual war going on, and it is being conducted in the soul of every believer, of every parish and diocese, in the world-wide church, and in the culture at large. If we are not aware that there is a war going on, our pastoral charity will tend to descend into tepidity and lukewarmness. The approach of John Vianney will seem strange and irrelevant.[40] The approach of Jesus, truly incomprehensible, is why there are so many efforts being made to silence the Gospel, edit the Gospel, put challenging parts of the Gospel in "brackets" so people will not be disturbed. This neutering of Jesus has got to stop. Aslan is not a tame lion.

As Pope Emeritus Benedict XVI has put it:

> A Jesus who agrees with everyone and everything, a Jesus without his holy anger, without the hardness of truth and genuine love is not the real Jesus as he is depicted in the Scriptures, but a pitiable caricature. A concept of "Gospel" that fails to convey the reality of God's anger has nothing to do with the Gospel of the Bible.[41]

Just consider one element of the spiritual armor that Paul considers so essential for the believer: the shield of faith, which is able to quench "all [the] flaming arrows of the evil one" (Eph 6:16).

None of us or our people are living in a neutral environment. All day long, the symbiotic work of the influence of the world culture, the drives of our disordered desires, and the direct temptations of the devil are at play in each person's soul. And yet, how many of us and our people are defenseless against these temptations? The shield of faith is composed of faith and complete trust in Jesus and knowledge of the objective content of the faith. So many of our people do not trust Him or know Him, and so many do not know His word, which is the foundation of true discernment and resistance to evil. There is a vicious war going on, and if people are not actively equipped with the spiritual armor, not just the shield of faith, they are likely to be captured or even enlisted in the enemy's campaign. And what about the shepherds, priests, and bishops who have stood mute while their sheep were carried off by the enemy to, in turn, become enemies themselves as they disdain the teaching of the Church and the authority of its clergy, often becoming vocal supporters of the devil's agenda as it pertains to abortion, homosexuality, and so on? I am very fearful for the salvation of many of our shepherds who are going to have to give an account to God about whether they were good shepherds or cowardly shepherds, or even conniving shepherds, as we all will have to according to our responsibilities.

In order to equip our people for the situation they are really facing, we need to be vigorous in our teaching and preaching, including the correction of error, admonishment of public sinners, and confrontation with the "wolves" that both Jesus and the Apostles prophesy will be a problem that emerges from within the Church in false teachers and prophets. At the moment, our formation of seminarians is not really preparing the future priests to conduct this vigorous dimension of their pastoral ministry, nor is our continuing formation of priests and the topics selected for clergy convocations and study days. The good shepherd has to protect his flock from the sheep and show no mercy to the wolves, and not tolerate a "Jezebel" in the midst of the flock. Too often, the wolves are welcome and even given pastoral assignments, and people are afraid to confront "Jezebel," thereby allowing the flock to be misled.

The prophetic participation in Jesus's ministry also has to include the deeds that back up the words. We have so many nice words and nice documents in the Church today but very little implementation and action. Paul's exhortations in the Pastoral Epistles to his pastoral collaborators and subordinates would make a good guide for our formation in pastoral ministry. But are we able to "receive" his exhortations given the psychological conditioning we are undergoing not to vigorously resist evil? Are we forming people who are able to receive and follow Paul's guidance on being a minister of the Gospel in difficult times?

I charge you in the presence of God and of Christ Jesus, who will judge the living and the dead, and by his appearing and his kingly power: proclaim the word; be persistent whether it is convenient or inconvenient; convince, reprimand, encourage through all patience and in teaching. For the time will come when people will not tolerate sound doctrine but, following their own desires and insatiable curiosity, will accumulate teachers and will stop listening to the truth and will be diverted to myths. But you, be self-possessed in all circumstances; put up with hardship; perform the work of an evangelist, fulfill your ministry. (2 Tm 4:1-5)

And what are we to make of Paul's admonition: "Reprimand publicly those who do sin, so that the rest also will be afraid" (1 Tim 5:20)? Is anybody being reprimanded publicly? Is anyone afraid to sin? Sometimes, this admonishing may need to be done formally and authoritatively as the many exhortations in the Pastoral Epistles to "command" things indicate. Sometimes, these admonitions need to be done informally and gently. "A slave of the Lord should not quarrel, but should be gentle with everyone, able to teach, tolerant, correcting opponents with kindness. It may be that God will grant them repentance that leads to knowledge of the truth, and that they may return to their senses out of the devil's snare, where they are entrapped by him, for his will" (2 Tm 2: 24-26).

All four dimensions of formation work together, of course. Participation in the prophetic mission of Jesus brings with it a zeal and a fervor that will inform every part of the priestly vocation. Pastoral charity that contains within it zeal and fervor will be willing to get up in the middle of the night to help the dying, will be diligent to make sure those in nursing homes are cared for, will be available for confession at convenient hours for people, will be fervent in preaching, will tell the truth to people in counseling, will prepare for the sacraments in a way that leads to conversion, and will reach out to the "lost" knowing that many are truly "lost." The whole priestly vocation and the central mission of the Church is nothing less than eternal life—or eternal death.

The Church is going through a profound purification right now. Widespread sin and corruption is being revealed, and deep repentance and reform is necessary. But this is not just a purification but a test. All of us are being put to the test to see if we are worthy of being called disciples of Jesus. Whether this is the "final confrontation" that Saint John Paul II spoke of,[42] or the severe test that Servais Pinckaers warned us of,[43] only time will tell. All of us now need to examine our consciences and prayerfully reflect on whether we are manifesting in our life and words the prophetic identify of Jesus to which all of us have been conformed. Do we fear God more than man? Are we zealous for the holiness of God's house, the Church, and for the salvation of souls? Are we passing on faithfully what He has asked us to preach and teach?

The Church in its turn must pass through the testing of faith, must stand alone before God far from the world, in order to be rooted in Christ, in God. These are the questions asked: will the Church dare to believe in the Word of God, even when it seems to be folly, a scandal, the stupidity of a prescientific age in the eyes of the world's learned ones? Will it have the courage to hope in God when human hope is gone, and renounce human support if need be? Can it love God more than the world and all it offers, more than itself . . . The crucial point in the encounter between Christianity and the modern world is found in the affirmation and audacious preaching of the supernatural, other-worldly character of faith in Jesus Christ . . . In the measure in which it avoids detachment and the transcendence of human values in order to remain bonded to the world . . . Whatever upheavals, illusions, books it may produce, it is self-condemned to spiritual sterility. It recoils before the cross of Christ.[44]

May God help us! He will if we want Him to.

NOTES

1.   One indication of the reduction of the priest's sharing in the prophetic mission of Jesus to simply teaching is found in the opening paragraph of the *Decree on the Ministry and Life of Priests* (*Presbyterorum Ordinis*): "Through the sacred ordination and mission which they receive from the bishops priests are promoted to the service of Christ the Teacher, Priest and King." Reducing the prophetic office of Christ to teaching is a severe reduction. The English is not a mistranslation as the Latin original is "*Christo Magistro, Sacerdoti et Regi.*" The reduction of the prophetic ministry of Christ is consistently reduced to teaching throughout the document (see section 13). In a similar way, the *Decree on the Pastoral Office of the Bishops in the Church* (*Christus Dominus*) exclusively refers to the teaching responsibilities of the bishops with not a word about the more comprehensive configuring to the prophetic mission of Jesus.

2.   There is a large and growing literature speaking of the change in focus among the Church's ministers that is needed in order to address the current cultural situation of declining Church membership and the growing numbers of the "nons." Among the most influential are: James Mallon, *Divine Renovation: Bringing Your Parish from Maintenance to Mission* (New London, CT: Twenty Third Publications, 2014); Archbishop Allen Vigneron, *Unleash the Gospel* (Available at www.aod.org); Steven Boguslawski, Ralph Martin, eds. *The New Evangelization: Overcoming the Obstacles* (Mahwah, NJ: Paulist, 2008); Ralph Martin, Peter Williamson, eds., *John Paul II and the New Evangelization* (Ann Arbor: Servant/St. Anthony, 2006); Robert Rivers, *From Maintenance to Mission: Evangelization and the Revitalization of the Parish* (Mahwah, NJ: Paulist Press, 2005); Michael White and Tom Corcoran, *Rebuilt: Awakening the Faithful, Reaching the Lost, Making Church Matter* (Notre Dame, IN: Ave Maria Press, 2013); Sherry Weddell, *Forming Intentional Disciples: The Path to Knowing and Following Jesus* (Huntington, IN: Our Sunday Visitor, 2012).

3.   This obviously has implications for the coordination of priestly leadership gifts that is the responsibility of the bishop but also for the pastor's coordination of lay leadership gifts in the parish. This is an important topic but one that is beyond the scope of this book.

4.   See Acts of the Apostles 10:34; 11:12.

5. At the same time, it is hard to overemphasize the prophetic nature of Jesus's mission. In fact, a respected Dominican scholar has written a convincing book claiming that the parallels between the prophet Elijah and Jesus are key to understanding His ministry. Paul Hinnebusch, O.P. *Jesus, The New Elijah* (Ann Arbor: Servant Books, 1978).

6. See Acts 7:37.

7. See also Matthew 13:57; Mark 6:4; John 4:43-44.

8. See Matthew 7:28-29; Luke 4:32.

9. See John 8:31-57.

10. See John 6:60-67.

11. See Matthew 23.

12. See John 17:14-18.

13. See Matthew 16:23; Mark 8:33.

14. See Psalm 69:10.

15. The underlying Greek word for "immorality" in this text, and in other texts as well, is *porneia*, which actually means sexual immorality. A new translation of the *New American Bible* is underway, and people working on the translation tell me that "immorality" will now be translated more accurately as "sexual immorality."

16. See also Luke 17:2.

17. See Peter Kreeft, *Jesus Shock* (Houston: Wellspring, 2012).

18. I use the term "salvation of souls" in full cognizance of contemporary theological anthropology that emphasizes the salvation of the whole person; but the fact remains that the soul is separated from the body at death and at that moment is judged, either saved or lost, only at the final judgement to be reunited with its body at the general resurrection.

19. Thomas Aquinas, *Summa Theologiae* I: II Q. 28, Art. 4. I am grateful to Monsignor Daniel Trapp, Spiritual Director of the Theologate at Sacred Heart Major Seminary, for reading an earlier draft of this book and suggesting the reference to St. Thomas.

20. See Luke 19:41.

21. I have devoted considerable effort to exploring and clarifying these questions. For a detailed account of the development of doctrine on this point and its mature formulation in Vatican II, see: Ralph Martin, *Will Many Be Saved? What Vatican II Actually Teaches and its Implications for the New Evangelization* (Grand Rapids: Eerdmans, 2012). For a more popular treatment, see Ralph Martin, *The Urgency of the New Evangelization: Answering*

the Call (Huntington: Our Sunday Visitor, 2013). See also: Ralph Martin "Considering Culpability," *Homiletic and Pastoral Review* (July 2017).

22. Paul VI, *Lumen Gentium* (1964), sec. 14.

23. The above material on the broad way and the narrow way and the teaching of Vatican II is taken from material developed for my book, *Will Many Be Saved? What Vatican II Actually Teaches and Its Implications for the New Evangelization* published by Eerdmans in 2012, which I have used in a variety of more popular articles and publications since then.

24. See www.lifesitenews.com/blogs/theologians-condemn-pope-benedicts-letter-on-abuse-crisis-on-german-bishops-website (Accessed April 20, 2019).

25. Fr. Andrew Apostoli, C.F.R., *Fatima for Today: The Urgent Marian Message of Hope* (San Francisco: Ignatius Press, 2010), 145.

26. In my opinion, the most reasonable understanding about who to fear is that it is both the devil, who can deceive us and lead us to hell, and God, who can judge unrepentant wrongdoing and condemn us to hell. A fear of hell, while disdained today as a motivation for turning to God, is not disdained by some of the greatest saints and spiritual writers in the history of the Church, not to mention Jesus Himself. While the goal is perfect love, the fear of hell has often been the necessary start for many.

27. "'I Haven't Killed Anyone' (What Serious Sins Will Exclude Us from the Kingdom of God?" *Homiletic and Pastoral Review* (December 2013).

28. Timothy Cardinal Dolan, "All Are Welcome," (blog), April 25, 2013, http://cardinaldolan.org/index.php/all-are-welcome/.

29. Paul VI, *Dei Verbum* (1965), sec. 11. For a fine selection of scholarly essays on the question of the inspiration and inerrancy of Scripture, see *For the Sake of Our Salvation: The Truth and Humility of God's Word*, ed. Scott Hahn (Steubenville, OH: St. Paul Center for Biblical Theology, 2010). Volume 6 in the series Letter and Spirit.

30. Augustine, *Contra Faustum* 17:3.

31. See my article, "Why Are We So Afraid to be Afraid of Hell," *National Catholic Register* (October 31, 2013).

32. This is an excerpt from a letter that St. Francis Xavier wrote to St. Ignatius of Loyola from India (E Vita Francisci Xaverii, auctore H. Tursellini, Romae, 1956, Lib. 4, epist. 4 [1542] et 5 [1544]). It is easily found in the Office of Readings for the feast day of St. Francis Xavier on December 3. Another accessible citation of this text is found in: Georg

Schurhammer, S.J., *Francis Xavier, His Life and His Times*, II (Chicago: Loyola Press, 1980), 407.

33. *Fatima in Lucia's own words: Sr. Lucia's Memoirs*, 21st edition, July 2017, ed. Fr. Louis Kondor, S.V.D.; trans. Dominican Nuns of Perpetual Rosary (Fundacao Francisco E Jacinta Marto, Fatima: July 2007), 78.

34. Ibid.

35. Ibid., 79.

36. Apostoli, *Fatima for Today*, 60.

37. Ibid., 66.

38. Ibid., 127.

39. "The Inner Ring" was the Memorial Lecture at King's College, University of London, in 1944, https://www.lewissociety.org/innerring/ (Accessed April 23, 2019).

40. See the essay by Monsignor John Cihak: *St. John Vianney's Pastoral Plan*, http://www.courageouspriest.com/father-john-cihak-saint-john-vianneys-pastoral-plan (Accessed October 30, 2018). See also, Jean Baptiste Marie Vianney, *Sermons for the Sundays and Feasts of the Year* (Long Prairie, MN: The Neumann Press, 1984).

41. Pope Benedict XVI. "Forgiveness as the Restoration of Truth," *Co-Workers of the Truth: Meditations for Every Day of the Year* (San Francisco, CA: Ignatius Press, 1992).

42. "The Final Confrontation," *Homiletic and Pastoral Review*, January 2017 edition (published December 20, 2016).

43. Servais Pinckaers, *The Sources of Christian Ethics*, trans. Sr. Mary Thomas Noble, 3rd Edition (Washington, DC: Catholic University of America Press, 1995), 313-315.

44. Ibid.